Charles Godfrey Leland

Hans Breitmann in church

With other ballads

Charles Godfrey Leland

Hans Breitmann in church
With other ballads

ISBN/EAN: 9783741181627

Manufactured in Europe, USA, Canada, Australia, Japa

Cover: Foto ©Angelika Wolter / pixelio.de

Manufactured and distributed by brebook publishing software
(www.brebook.com)

Charles Godfrey Leland

Hans Breitmann in church

Price 1s.

Hans Breitmann's Party.

With other Ballads.

CONTENTS.

Hans Breitmann

IN

Church.

With other Ballads.

BY

CHARLES G. LELAND.

LONDON:
TRÜBNER & CO., 60 PATERNOSTER ROW.
1870.

EDITOR'S PREFACE.

THE Editor has pleasure in being at length enabled to publish a new series of "Breitmann Ballads," and does so, in the hope that these latest poems will sustain the high reputation gained for the author by his previous labours in the same field of poetry.

As regards some of the points and incidents of the poems contained in this volume, the following remarks may not be inappropriate.

The ballad, "Breitmann's Going to Church," is based on a real occurrence. A certain colonel, with his men, did really, during the war, go to a church in or near Nashville, and, as the saying is, "kicked up the devil, and broke things," to such an extent, that a serious reprimand from the colonel's superior officer was the result. The fact is guaranteed by Mr Leland, who heard the offender complain of the "cruel and heartless stretch of military authority." As regards the firing into the guerilla ball-room, it took place near Murfreesboro', on the night of Feb. 10 or 11, 1865; and on the next day, Mr Leland was at a house where one of the wounded lay. On the same night a Federal picket was shot dead near Lavergne; and the next night a detachment of cavalry was sent off from General Van Cleve's quarters, the officer in command coming in while the author was talking with the general, for final orders. They rode twenty miles that night, attacked a body of guerillas, captured a number, and brought back prisoners early next day. The same day Mr Leland, with a small cavalry escort, and a few friends, went out into the country, during which ride one or two curious incidents occurred, illustrating the extraordinary fidelity of the blacks to Federal soldiers.

V

The explanation of the poem entitled, "The First Edition of Breitmann," is as follows :—It was not long after the war that a friend of the writer's to whom "The Breitmann Ballads" had been sent in MSS., and who had frequently urged the former to have them published, resolved to secure, at least, a small private edition, though at his own expense. Unfortunately the printers quarreled about the MSS., and, as the writer understood, the entire concern broke up in a row in consequence. And, in fact, when we reflect on the amount of fierce attack and recrimination which this unpretending and peaceful little volume elicited after the appearance of the fifth English edition, the injury which it sustained from garbled and falsified editions, and an unauthorised Australian reprint, it would really seem as if this first edition, which "died a borning," had been typical of the stormy path to which the work was predestined.

"I Gili Romaneskro," a gipsy ballad, was written both in the original and translation—that is to say, in the German gipsy and German English dialects—to cast a new light on the many-sided Bohemianism of Herr Breitmann. "Steinli von Slang" is simply a lay or a ballad amplified to a romance. The lines "To a Friend Studying German," may be, we believe, appropriately enough addressed to any lady or gentleman employed in mastering the mighty and mysterious head of the Teutonic branches. For the author having been assured that great numbers of this book were bought to present, in the way of a jest, to friends devoted to the study of German, it occurred to him that a poem devoted to this subject would not be unacceptable.

With the exception of a few verses in one poem all the ballads contained in this volume were written in Europe.

LONDON, *January* 20, 1870.

BREITMANN'S GOING TO CHURCH.

"Vides igitur, Collega carissime, visitationem canonicam esse rem haud ita periculosam, sed valde amoenam, si modo vinum, groggio et cibi praesto sunt."

—*Novissimae Epistolae Obscurorum Virorum, Berolini F. Berggold*, 1869. *Epistola* xxiii., p. 63.

D'VAS near de state of Nashfille,
In de town of Tennessee,
Der Breitmann vonce vas quarderd
Mit all his cavallrie.
Der Sheneral kept him glose in gamp,
He vould'nt let dem go ;
Dey couldn't shdeal de first plack hen,
Or make de red cock crow.

Und virst der Breitmann vildly shmiled,
  Und denn he madly shvore ;
Crate h—l, mit shpoons und shinsherbread
  Can *dis* pe makin war?
Verdammt pe all der discipline !
  Verdammt der Shenerál !
Vere I vonce on de road, his will,
  Vere wurst mir und egâl.

" Oh vhere ish all de plazin roofs
  Dat claddened vonce mine eyes?
Und vhere de crand plantaschions
  Vhere ve gaddered many a brize?
Und vhere de plasted shpies ve hung
  A howlin loud mit fear?
Und vhere de rascal push-whackers
  Ve shashed like vritened deer?

" De roofs are shtandin fast and firm
Mit repels blottin oonder ;
De crand blantaschions lie round loose
For Morgan's men to ploonder !
De shpies go valkin out und in,
Ash sassy ash can pe ;
Und in de voods de push-whackers
Are makin foon of me !

" Oh vere I on my schimmel grey
Mein sabre in mein hand,
Dey should drack me py de ruins
Of de houses troo de land.
Dey should drack me py de puzzards
High sailen ofer head,
A vollowin der Breitmann's trail
To claw de repel dead."

Outspoke der bold Von Stossenheim,
  Who had théories of Gott:
"O Breitmann, dis ish shoodgement on
  De vays dat you hafe trot.
You only lifes to joy yourself,
  Yet you, yourself moost say,
Dat self-defelopment requires
  De réligiös Idée."

Dey sat dem down und argued id,
  Like Deutschers vree from fear,
Dill dey schmoke ten pfounds of knaster,
  Und drinked drei fass of bier.
Der Breitmann go py Schopenhauer,
  Boot Veit he had him denn;
For he dook him on de angles
  Of de moral oxygen.

Der Breitmann 'low, dat 'pentence,
Ish known in efery glime,
Und dat to grin und bear it
Vas healty und sooplime.
" For mine Sout German Catolicks,
Id vas pe goot, I know;
Likevise dem Nordland Luterans,
If vonce to shoorsh dey go.

" Boot how vas id mit oders,
Who dinks philosophie?
I don't begreif de matter,"
Said Stossenheim: " Denn see.
De more dat shoorsh disgoostet you,
Und make despise und bain,
De crater merid ish to go,
Und de crater ish your gain."

"I know a liddle shoorsh mineself,
  Oopon de Bole Jack road :
(De rebs vonce shot dree Federals dere,
  Ash into shoorsh dey goed).
Dere you might make a bilcrimage,
  Und do id in a tay :
Gott only knows vot dings you mighdt
  Bick oop, oopon de vay."

Denn oop dere shpoke a contrapand,
  Vas at de tent id's toor—
"Dere's twenty bar'ls of whiskey, hid,
  In dat tabernacle, shore.
A rebel he done gone and put
  It in de cellar, true,
No libin man dat secret knows,
  'Cept only me an' you."

Der Stossenheim, he grossed himself,
  Und knelt peside de fence,
Und gried : " O Coptain Breitmann, see,
  Die finger Providence."
Der Breitmann doed his hat afay,
  Says he, " Pe 't hit or miss,
I 'fe heard of miragles pefore,
  Boot none so hunk ash dis."

" Wohlauf mine pully cafaliers,
  Ve 'll ride to shoorsh to-day,
Each man ash hasn't cot a horse
  Moost shteal von, rite afay.
Dere 's a raw, green corps from Michigan,
  Mit horses on de loose,
You men ash vants some hoof-irons,
  Look out und crip deir shoes."

All brooshed und fixed, de cavallrie
  Rode out py moonen shine,
De cotton fields in shimmerin light,
  Lay white as elfenbein.
Dey heard a shot close py Lavergne,
  Und men who rode afay,
In de road a-velterin in his ploot,
  A Federal picket lay.

Und all dat he hafe dimes to say,
" Vhile shtandin at my post,
De guerillas got first shot at me,"
  Und so gafe oop de ghost.
Denn a contrapand, who helt his head,
  Said : " Sah—dose grillers all
Is only half a mile from hy'ar,
  A dancin at a ball."

Der Breitmann shpoke and brummed it out
  Ash if his heart tid schvell :
" I 'll gife dem music at dat pall
  Vill tantz dem indo hell."
Hei !—arrow-fast—a teufel's ride !
  De plack man led de vay,
Dey reach de house—dey see de lights—
  Dey heard de fiddle blay.

Dey nefer vaited for a word
  Boot galloped from de gloom,
Und, bang !—a hoonderd carpine shots
  Dey fired indo de room.
Oop vent de groans of vounded men,
  De fittlin died away :
Boot some of dem vere tead pefore
  De music ceased to blay.

Denn crack und smack coom scotterin shots
  Troo vindow und troo door,
Boot bang and clang de Germans gife
  Anoder volley more.
"Dere—let 'em shlide. Right file to shoorsh!"
  Aloudt de orders ran.
"I kess I paid dem for dat shot,"
  Shpeak grim der Breitemann.

All rosen red de mornin fair
  Shone gaily o'er de hill,
All violet plue de shky crew teep
  In rifer, pond, und rill;
All cloudy grey de limeshtone rocks
  Coom oop troo dimmerin wood;
All shnowy vite in mornin light
  De shoorsh pefore dem shtood.

"Now loudet vell de organ, oop,
To drill mit solemn fear;
Und ring also dat Lumpenglock
To pring de beoples here.
Und if it prings guerillas down,
Ve 'll gife dem, py de Lord,
De low-mass of de sabre, and
De high-mass of de cord.

"Du, Eberlé aus Freiburg,
Du bist ein Musikant,
Top-sawyer on de counterpoint
Und buster in discánt,
To dee de soul of musik
All innerly ish known,
Du canst mit might fullenden
De art of orgel-ton."

"Derefore, a Miserére
  Vilt dou, be-ghostet, spiel,
Und vake be-raiséd yearnin,
  Also a holy feel :—
Pe referent, men—rememper
  Dis ish a Gotteshaus—
Du Conrad—go along de aisles
  Und schenk de whiskey aus!"

Dey blay crate dings from Mozart,
  Beethoven und Méhul,
Mit chorals of Sebastian Bach
  Sooplime and peaudiful.
Der Breitmann feel like holy saints,
  De tears roon down his fuss ;
Und he sopped out, "Gott verdammich—dis
  Ist wahres Kunstgenuss!"*

* Is true art-enjoyment.

Der Eberlé blayed oop so high,
He maket de rafters ring
Der Eberlé blayed lower, und
Ve heardt der Breitmann sing
Like a dronin wind in piney woods,
Like a nightly moanin sea :
Ash de dinked on Sonntags long agone
Vhen a poy in Germany.

Und louder und mit louder tone
High oop de orgel blowed,
Und plentifuller efer yet
Around de whiskey goed.
Dey singed ash if mit singin, dey
Might indo Himmel win :—
I dink in all dis land soosh shprees
Ash yet hafe nefer peen.

Vhen in de Abendsonnenschein,
  Mit doost-clouds troo de door,
All plack ash night in golden lighdt
  Dere shtood ein schwartzer Mohr,
Dat contrapand so wild und weh,
  Mit eye-palls glaring roun,
Who cried "For Gott's sake, hoory oop!
  De reps ish gomin down!"

Und while he yet was shpeakin,
  A far-off soundt pegan,
Down rollin from de moundain
  Of many a ridersmann.
Und vhile de waves of musik
  Vere rollin o'er deir heads,
Dey heard a foice a schkreemin,
  "Pile out of thar, you Feds!

" For we uns ar' a comin
For to guv to you uns fits,
And knock you into brimstun
And blast you all to bits"——
Boot ere it done ids shpeakin,
Der vas order in de band,
Ash Breitmann, mit an awfool stim
Out-dondered his gommand.

Und ash fisch-hawk at a mackarel
Doth make a splurgin flung,
Und ash eagles dab de fish-hawks
Ash if de gods vere young.
So from all de doors and vindows,
Like shpiders down deir webs
De Dootch went at deir horses,
Und de horses at de rebs.

Crate shplendors of de treadful
  Vere in dat pattle rush,
Crate vights mit swords und carpine,
  Py efery fence and bush.
Ash panters vight mit crislies
  In famished morder fits—
For de rebs vere mad ash boison
  Und de Dootch vere droonk ash blitz.

Yet vild ash vas dis pattle,
  So quickly vas it o'er,
O, vhy moost I forefer
  Pestain mine page mit gore?
Py liddle und py liddle
  Dey drawed demselfs afay,
Oft toornin' round to vighten
  Like boofaloes at bay.

De scatterin shots grew fewer,
  De scatterin gries more shlow,
Und furder troo de forest
  Ve heared dem vainter grow.
Ve gife von shout—"Victoria !"
  Und denn der Breitmann said,
Ash he wiped his ploody sabre :
  "Now, poys, count oop your dead !"

Oh small had been our shoutin
  For shoy, if ve had known
Dat der Stossenheim im oaken wald,
  Lay dyin all alone.
Vhile his oldt vhite horse mit droopin het
  Look dumbly on him doun,
Ash if he dinked, "Vy lyest dou here
  Vhile fightin's goin on ?"

Und dreams coom o'er de soldier
  Slow dyin on de eart;
Of a schloss afar in Baden,
  Of his mutter, und nople birt!
Of poverty and sorrow,
  Vhich drofe him like de wind,
Und he sighed, "Ach weh for de lofed ones,
  Who wait so far pehind!

"Wohl auf, my soul o'er de moundains!
  Wohl auf—well ofer de sea!
Dere's a frau dat sits in de Odenwald
  Und shpins, und dinks of me.
Dere's a shild ash blays in de greenin grass,
  Und sings a liddle hymn,
Und learns to shpeak a fader's name
  Dat she nefer will shpeak to him.

" But mordal life ends shortly
  Und Heafen's life is long :—
Wo bist du Breitmann ?—glaub'es—*
  Gott suffers noding wrong.
Now I die like a Christian soldier,
  My head oopon my sword :—
In nomine Domini !"—
  Vas Stossenheim his word.

O, dere vas bitter wailen
  Vhen Stossenheim vas found.
Efen from dose dere lyin
  Fast dyin on de ground.
Boot time vas short for vaiten,
  De shades vere gadderin dim :
Und I nefer shall forget it
  De hour ve puried him.

* Where are thou Breitmann ?—Believe it.

De tramp of horse und soldiers
  Vas all de funeral knell;
De ring of sporn und carpine
  Vas all de sacrin bell.
Mit hoontin knife und sabre
  Dey digged de grave a span
From German eyes blue gleamin
  De holy water ran.

Mit moss-grown shticks und bark-thong
  De plessed cross ve made,
Und put it vhere de soldier's head
  Towards Germany vas laid.
Dat grave is lost mid dead leafs
  De cross is goned afay:
Boot Gott will find der reiter
  Oopon de Youngest Day.

Und dinkin of de fightin,
  Und dinkin of de dead,
Und dinkin of de organ,
  To Nashville, Breitmann led.
Boot long dat rough oldt Hanserl
  Vas earnsthaft, grim und kalt,
Shtill dinkin o'er de hearts friend,
  He 'd left im gruenen wald.*

De verses of dis boem
  In Heidelberg I write
De night is dark around me
  De shtars apove are bright.
Studenten in den Gassen †
  Make singen many a song ;

* In the green wood.
† Students in the streets.

Ach Faderland !—wie bist du weit !
Ach Zeit !—wie bist du lang ! *

* Oh Fatherland !—how art thou far.
Oh Time ! -how art thou long.

THE FIRST EDITION OF BREITMANN.

SHOWING HOW AND WHY IT WAS THAT IT NEVER APPEARED.

" Uns ist in alten Maeren
  wunders viel geseit
Von Helden lobebaeren,
  von grosser Arebeit.
Von Festen und Hochzeiten,
  von Weinen und Klagen,
Von kuehnen Recken Streiten,
  möht Ihr nun Wunder hören sagen."

—Der Nibelungen Lied.

DO oos, in anciend shdory,
  Crate voonders ish peen told
Of lapors fool of glory,
  Of heroes bluff und bold ;

Of high oldt times a-kitin,
  Of howlin und of tears,
Of kissin and of vightin,
  All dis we likes to hears.

Dere growed once dimes in Schwaben,
  Since fifty years pegan,
An shild of decend elders,
  His name Hans Breitemann.
De gross adfentures dat he had,
  If you will only look,
Ish all bescribed so truly
  In dis fore-lying book.

Und allaweil dese lieder
  Vere goin troo his het,
De writer lay von Sonntay
  A-shleepin in his bett ;

Vhen, lo ! a yellow bigeon
  Coom to him in a dream,
De same dat Mr Barnum
  Vonce had in his Muséum.

Und dus out-shprach de bigeon :
  " If you should brint de songs
Or oder dings of Breitmann
  Vhich to dem on-belongs,
Dey will tread de road of Sturm and Drang,
  Die wile es möhte leben,*
Und be mis-geborn in pattle—
  To dis fate ish it ergeben."

Und dus rebly de dreamer :
  " If on de ice it shlip,
Denn led id dake ids shanses,
  Rip Sam, und let 'er rip !

* During its life.

Dou say'st id vill pe sturmy:
  Vot sturmy ish, ish crand,
Crates heroes ish de beoples
  In Uncle Samuel's land.

"Du bist ein rechter Gelbschnabel,*
  O golden bigeon mine,
Und I'll fighdt id on dis summer,
  If id dakes me all dis line.
Full liddle ish de discount,
  Oopon de Yankee peeps."
"Go to hell!" exglaim de bigeon;
  Foreby vas all mine shleeps.

Dere vent to Sout Carolina
  A shentleman who dinked,
Dat te pallads of der Breitmann
  Should papered pe und inked.

* Thou art a very puppy.

Und dat he vouldt fixed de brintin
  Before de writer know :
Dis make to many a brinter,
  Fool many a bitter woe.

All in de down of Charleston,
  A druckerei he found,
Where dey cut de copy into *takes*
  Und sorted it around. !
Und all vas goot peginnen,
  For no man heeded mooch,
Dat half de jours vas Mericans
  Und half of dem vas Dutch.

Und vorser shtill, anoder half
  Had vorn de Federal plue,
Vhile de anti-half in Davis grey
  Had peen Confeterates true.

Great Himmel! vot a shindy
  Vas shdarted in de crowd,
Vhen some von read Hans Breitmann,
  His Barty all aloud!

Und von goot-nadured Yankee,
  He schwear id vos a shame,
To dell soosh lies on Dutchmen,
  Und make of dem a game.
Boot dis make mad Fritz Luder,
  Und he schwear dis treat of Hans,
Vos shoost so goot a barty
  Ash any oder man's.

Und dat nodings vas so looscious
  In all dis eartly shpear,
Ash a quart mug fool of sauer-kraut,
  Mit a plate of Lager-bier.

Dat de Yankee might pe tam mit himself,
  For he der Fritz hafe peen,
In many soosh a barty
  Und all dose dings hafe seen.

All mad oopsproong de Yankee,
  Mit all his passion ripe;
Und vired at Fritz mit de shootin shtick,
  Vheremit he vas fixin type.
It hit him on de occiput,
  Und laid him on de floor;
For many a long day afder
  I ween his het was sore.

Dis roused Piet Weiser der Pfaelzer,
  Who vas quick to act und dink;
He held in hand a roller
  Vheremit he vas rollin ink.

Und he dake his broof py shtrikin
  Der Merican top of his het,
Und make soosh a vine impression,
  Dat he left de veller for deat.

Allaweil dese dings oonfolded,
  Dere vas rows of anoder kind,
Und drople in de wigwam
  Enough to trife dem plind.
Und a crate six-vooted Soudern man
  Vot hafe vorked on a Refiew,
Shvear he hope to Gott he mighd pie de forms
  If de Breitmann's book war'nt true.

For de Sout' vas ploundered derriple,
  Und in dat darksome hour
He hafe lossed a yallow-pine maiden,
  Of all de land de vlower.

Bright gold doublones a hoondered
For her he'd gladly bay
Ash soon ash a thrip for a ginger-cake,
Und deem it cheap dat day.

To him antworded a Yorker
Who shoomp den dimes de *boun-ti-ee:*
(De only dings *he* lossed in de war
Was a sense of broperty).
Says he, "Votefer you hafe dropped
Some oder shap hafe get,
Und de yallow pine liked him petter ash you,
On dat it is safe to bet!"

Dead pale pecame dat Soudern brave
He tidn't so moosh as yell,
Boot he drop right on to de Yorker,
Und mit von lick bust his shell.

Denn out he flashed his pig-sticker
  Und mit looks of drementous gloom,
Rooshed vildly in de pattle
  Dat vas ragin round de room.

Boot *in angulo*, in de corner—
  Anoder quarrel vas grow
'Twix a Boston shap mit a Londoner;
  Und de row ish gekommen so:
De Yankee say dat de H-*u*-mor
  Of Breitmann vas less dan small,
Dough he maket de beoples laughen,
  Boot dat vas only all.

Denn a Deutscher say by Donner!
  Dat soosh a baradox
Vould leafe no hope for writers
  In all Pandora's bænder box.

'Twas like de sayin dat Heine
   Hafe no witz in him goot or bad,
Boot he only *kept sayin* witty dings
   To make beoples pelieve he had.

Denn de oder veller be-headed
   Dat dere vas not a shbark of foon
In de Breitmann lieds when you lead dem
   Into Englisch correctly done :—
Den a Proof Sheet veller respondered,
   For he dink de dings vas hard,
" Dat ish shoost like de goot oldt lady
   Ash vent to hear Artemus Ward."

" Und say it vas shames de beoples
   Vas laugh demselfs most tead
At de boor young veller lecturin,
   Vhen he tidn't know vot he said."

Hereauf de Yankee answered
" Gaul dern it:—Shtop your fuss!"
And all de crowd togeder
  Go slap in a grand plug-muss.

De Yankee shlog de Proof Sheet
  Soosh an awfool smock on de face
Dat he shvell rite oop like a poonkin
  Mit a sense of his tisgrace,
Boot der Deutscher boosted an ink-keg
  On dop of de oder's hair:
It vly troo de air like a boomshell—denn
  Mine Gotts!—Vot a sighdt vas dere!

Denn ofer all de shapel
  Vierce war vas ragin loose;
Fool many a vighten brinter
  Got well ge-gooked his goose.

Fool many a nose mit fisten,
  I ween was padly scrouged ;
Fool many an eye pright gleamin
  Vas ploody out-gegouged.

*Dô wart ûfgehouwen,**
  Dere vas hewin off of pones ;
*Dô hôrte man darinne**
  Man heardt soosh treadful croans.
*Jach waren dâ die Geste,**
  De row vas rough and tough,
Genuoge sluogen wunden—*
  Dere vas plooty wounds enough.

De souls of anciend brinters
  From Himmel look down oopon,
Und allowed dat in a *chapel*
  Dere was nefer soosh carryins on.

* Lines from Gudrun.

Dere was Lorenz Coster mit Gutemberg,
  Und Scheffer mit der Fust,
Und Sweynheim mit Pannartz trop deers,
  Oopon dis teufel's dust.

Dere vas Yankee jours extincted
  Who lay upon the vloor,
Dere vas Soudern rebs destructed,
  Who vouldt nefer Jeff no more.
Ash deir souls rise oop to Heafen,
  Dey heardt de oldt brinters' calls,
Und Gutemberg gifed dem all a kick
  Ash he histed dem ofer de walls.

Dat ish de vay dese Ballads
  Foorst vere crooshed in ploot and shdorm,
Fool many a day moost bass afay
  Pefore dey dook dis form.

De copy flootered o'er de preasts
  Of heroes lyin todt,
Dis vas de dire peginnin—
  Das war des Breitmann's Noth.

Dis song in Philadelphia
  Long dimes ago pegun,
In Paris vas gondinued, und
  In Dresden ist full-done.
If any toubt apout de *facts*,
  In nople minds ish grew,
Let dem ashk Carl Benson Bristed,
  He knows id all ish drue.

Und now, dese Breitmann shdories
  Is gebrindt in many a lant,
Sogar in far Australia
  Dey 're gestohlen und bekannt :—

"Geh hin mein Puch in alle VVelt
Steh auss was dir kompt zu!
Man beysse Dich, man reysse Dich
Nur dass man mir nichts thu! *

* Go forth my book through all the world,
Bear what thy fate may be!
They may bite thee, they may tear thee,
So they do no harm to me!

I GILI ROMANESKRO.

A GIPSY BALLAD.

WHEN der Herr Breitmann vas a yungling, he vas go bummin aroundt goot deal in de worldt, vestigatin human natur, *roulant de vergne en vergne*, ash de Fraentsch boet says: "goin from town to town;" seein beobles in gemixed sociedy, und learnin dose languages vitch ornamendt a drue moskopolite, or von whose het ish bemosst mit experience. Mong oder tongues, ash it would appeared, he shpoke fluendly Red Welsh, Black Dootch, Kauder-Waelsch, Gauner-sprache und Shipsy; und dis latter languashe he pring so wide dat he write a pook of pallads in it, —von of vitch pallads I hafe intuce him mit moosh droples to telifer ofer to de worldt. De inclined reader vill, mit crate heavy-hood blace pefore himself de fexation und lapor I hafe hat in der Breitmann his absents, to ged dese Shipsy verses broperly gorrected; as de only shentleman in town who vas culpable of so doin, ish peen gonfined in de town-brison, pout some droples he hat for shdealin some hens; und pefore I couldt consoolt mit him, he vas rooned afay. Denn I fond an oldt vomans Shipsy, who vas do nodings boot peg, und so wider mit pout five or four oders more. Derfore, de errordoms moost pe excused py de enlightened pooplic, who are fomiliar mit dis peautiful longuashe, vitch is now so shenerally fashionábel in literary und shpordin circles.

I GILI ROMANESKRO.

Schunava, ke baschko dela godla,
Schunava Paschomàskro.
Te del miro Dewel tumen
Dschavena bachtallo.

Schunava opré to ruka
Chiriklô ke gillela :
Kamovéla but dives,
Eh'me pale kamaveva.

Apo je wa'wer divesseste
Schunava pro gilaviben,
M'akana me avava,
Pro marzos, pro kuriben.

So korava kuribente,
  So korava apre dróm ;
Me kanáv miri romni,
  So kamela la lákero rom.

DRANSLATION.

I hear de gock a growin !
  I hear de musikant !
Gott gife dee a happy shourney
  Vhen you go to a distand landt.

I hears oopon de pranches
  A pird mit merry shdrain,
Goot many tays moost fanish
  Ere I coom to dis blace again.

Oopon some oder tay-times
  I 'll hear dat song from dee ;
Boot now I goes ash soldier
  To war, o'er de rollin sea.

Und vot I shdeals in pattle,
  Und vot on de road I shdeal,
I 'll pring all to my true lofe
  Who lofes her loafer so well.

STEINLI VON SLANG.

I.

DER watchman look out from his tower
Ash de Abendgold glimmer grew dim,
Und saw on de road troo de Gauer
Ten shpearmen coom ridin to him :
Und he schvear : " May I lose my next bitter
Und denn mit der Teufel go hang !
If id isn't dat pully young Ritter,
De hell-drivin Steinli von Slang.

"De vorldt nefer had any such man,
He vights like a sturm in its wrath:
You may call me a recular Dutchman,
If he arn't like Goliath of Gath.
He ish big ash de shiant O'Brady,
More ash sefen feet high on a string,
Boot he can't vin de hearts of my lady,
De lofely Plectruda von Sling."

De lady make welcome her gast in
Ash he shtep to de dop of de shtair,
She look like an angel got lost in
A forest of autumn-prown hair.
Und a bower-maiden said ash she tarried:
"I wish I may bust mit a bang!
If id isn't a shame she ain't married
To der her-re-liche Steinli von Slang!"

He pows to de crouñd fore de lady,
  Vhile his vace ish ash pale ash de tead;
Und she vhispers oonto him a rédè
  Ash mit arrow point accents, she said:
"You hafe long dimes peen dryin to win me,
  You hafe vight, and mine braises you sing,
Boot I'm 'fraid dat de notion aint in me,
  De Lady Plectruda von Sling."

"Boot brafehood teserfes a reward, sir;
  Dough you've hardly a chost of a shanse.
Sankt Werolf! medinks id ish hard, sir,
  I should allaweil lead you dis dance.
Like a bees vhen it booz troo de clofer,
  Dese murmurin accents she flang,
Vhile singin, a stingin her lofer,
  Der woe-moody Ritter von Slang.

"Boot if von ding you do, I 'll knock under,
Our droples moost enden damit.
Und if you pull troo it,—by donder!
I 'll own myself euchred, und bit.
I schvear py de holy Sanct Chlody!
Py mine honor—und avery ding!
You may hafe me—soul, puttons, und pody,
Mit de whole of Plectruda von Sling."

"Und dis ish de test of your power:—
Vhile ve shtand ourselfs round in a row,
You moost roll from de dop of dis tower,
Down shdairs to de valley pelow.
Id ish rough and ash shteep ash my virtue:
(Mit schwanenshweet accents she sang:)
"Tont try if you dinks id vill hurt you
Mine goot liddle Ritter von Slang."

An moormoor arosed mong de beoples:
  In fain tid she doorn in her shkorn,
Der vatchman on dop of de shdeeples
  Plowed a sorryfool doon on his horn.
Ash dey look down de dousand-foot treppé,
  Dey schveared dey vouldt *pass* on de ding,
Und not roll down de firstest tam steppé
  For a hoondred like Fraulein von Sling.

II.

'Twas audumn. De dry leafs vere bustlin
  Und visperin deir elfin wild talk,
Vhen shlow, mit his veet in dem rustlin
  Herr Steinle coomed out for a walk.
Wild dooks vly afar in de gloamin,
  He hear a vaint gry vrom de gang;
Und vished he vere off mit dem roamin:
  De heart-wounded Ritter von Slang.

Und ash he vent musin und shbeakin,
He see, shoost ahead in his vay,
In sinkular manner a streakin,
A strange liddle bein, in cray,
Who toorned on him quick mit a holler,
Und cuttin a dwo bigeon ving,
Cried, "Say, can you change me a thaler,
Oh, guest of de Lady von Sling?"

De knight vas a goot-nadured veller,
(De peggars all knowed him at sight),
So he forked out each groschen und heller,
Dill he fix de finances aright.
Boot shoost ash de liddle man vent, he,
(Der Ritter), astonished cried "Dang!"
For id vasn't *von* thaler boot *tventy*,
He'd passed on der Ritter von Slang.

O reater! soopose soosh a vlight in
De vingers of *me*, or of *you*,
How we'd toorned on our heels, und gone kitin
Dill no von vos left to pursue!
Good Lort! how *we'd* froze to de ready!
Boot mit him 'dvas a different ding;
For *he* vent on de high, moral steady,
Dis lofer of Fräulein von Sling.

Und dough no von vill gife any gredit
To dis part of mine dale, shdill id 's drue,
He drafelled ash if he vould dead it,
Dis liddle oldt man to pursue.
Und loudly he after him hollers,
Till de vales mit de cliffers loud rang:
"You hafe gifed me nine-ten too moosh dollars,
Hold hard!" cried der Ritter von Slang.

De oldt man ope his eyes like a casement,
Und laidt a cold hand on his prow,
Denn mutter in ootmosdt amazement,
" Vot manner of mordal art dou ?
I hafe lifed in dis world a yar tausend,
Und nefer yed met soosh a ding !
Yet you find it hart vork to pe spouse, and
Peloved by Lady von Sling ! "

" Und she vant you to roll from de tower
Down shteps to yon rifulet shpot."
(Here de knight whom amazement oerbower,
Cried " Himmels potz pumpen Herr Gott ! ")
Boot de oldt veller saidt : " I 'll arrange it,
Let your droples und sorrows co hang !
Und no dings vill coom to derange it,
Pet high on it, Ritter von Slang.

"So get oop dis small oonderstandin,
 Dat to-morrow by ten, do you hear?
You 'll pe mit your *trunk* at de landin;
 I 'll also be dere—nefer fear!
Und I dinks we shall make your young voman
 A new kind of meloty sing;
Dat vain, wicked, cruel, unhuman,
 Gott-tamnaple Fräulein von Sling."

De fiolet shdars vere apofe him,
 Vhite moths und vhite dofes shimmered round,
All nature seemed seekin to lofe him,
 Mit perfume und vision und sound.
De liddle oldt veller hat fanished,
 In a harp-like, melotious twang;
Und mit him all sorrow vas panished
 Afay from der Steinli von Slang.

III.

Id vas morn, und de vorldt hat assempled
Mid panners und lances und dust,
Boot de heart of de Paroness trempled,
Und ofden her folly she cussed.
For she found dat der Ritter vould *do it*,
Und "die or get into de Ring,"
Und denn she 'd pe cerdain to rue it,
Aldough she vas Lady von Sling.

For no man in Deutschland stood higher
Dan he mit de Minnesing crew,
He vas friendet to Heini von Steier,
Und Wolfram von Eschenbach too.
Und she dinked ash she look from de vinders,
How herzlich his braises dey sang;
"Now dey 'll knock my goot name indo flinders,
For killin der Ritter von Slang."

Boot oh! der goot knight had a Schauer,
Und felt most ongommonly queer,
Vhen he find on de top of de dower
De goblum, pesite him, abbear.
Denn he find he no more could go valkin,
Und shtood, shoost an potrified ding,
Vhile de goblum vent round apout talkin,
Und chaffin Plectruda von Sling.

Denn at vonce he see indo de problum,
Und vas stoggered like rats at ids *vim*;
His soul had gone indo de goblum,
Und de goblum's hat gone indo him.
Und de eyes of de volk vas enchanted,
Dere vas "glamour" oopon de whole gang;
For dey dinked dat dis veller who ranted
So loose, vas der Ritter von Slang.

Und, Lordt! how he dalked! Oonder heafens
  Dere vas nefer soosh derriple witz,
Knockin all dings to sechses and sefens,
  Und gifin Plectruda, Dutch fits.
Mein Gott! how he poonished und chaffed her
  Like a hell-stingin, devil-born ding;
Vhile de volk lay a-rollin mit laughter
  At Fräulein Plectruda von Sling.

De lady grew angry und paler,
  De lady grew ratful und red,
She felt some Satanical jailer
  Hafe brisoned de tongue in her head.
She moost laugh vhen she vant to pe cryin.
  Und vas crushed mit de teufelisch clang,
Till she knelt herself, pooty near dyin,
  To dis derriple image of Slang.

Denn der goblum shoomp oop to der ceiling
  Und trow sommerseds round on de vloor,
Right ofer Plectruda a-kneelin,
  Dill she look more a vool dan pefore.
Denn he roll down de shteps light und breezy,
  His laughs made it all apout ring;
Ash he shveared dere vas noding more easy
  Dan to win a Plectruda von Sling.

Und vhen he cot down to de pottom,
  He laugh so to freezen your plood;
Und schwear dat de boomps ash he cot em
  Hafe make him feel petter ash good.
Boot, oh! how dey shook at his power,
  Vhen he toorned himself roundt mit a bang,
Und *roll oop* to de dop of de tower,
  To change forms mit de *oder* Von Slang!

Denn all in an insdand vas altered,
  Der Steine vas coom to himself;
Und de sprite, vitch in double sense paltered,
  From dat moment acain vas an elf.
Dey shdill dinked dat *he* vas de person
  Who had bobbed oop and down on de ving,
Und knew not who 'tvas lay de curse on
  De peaudiful Lady von Sling.

Nun—endlich—Plectruda repented,
  Und gazed on der Ritter mit shoy;
In dime to pe married consented,
  Und vas plessed mit a peautifool poy,
A dwenty gold biece on his bosom
  Vhen geporn vas tiscofered to hang
Mit de inscript—" Dis dime dont refuse em"—
  So endet de tale of Von Slang.

TO A FRIEND STUDYING GERMAN.

Si liceret te amare
Ad Suevorum magnum mare,
Sponsam te perducerem.
—*Tristicia Amorosa.* Frau Aventiure,
von J. V. Scheffel.

WILL'ST dou learn die Deutsche Sprache ?
Denn set it on your card,
Dat all the nouns have shenders,
Und de shenders all are hard.
Dere ish also dings called pronoms,
Vitch id's shoost ash vell to know ;
Boot ach ! de verbs or time-words—
Dey'll work you bitter woe.

Will'st dou learn de Deutsche Sprache?
  Denn you allatag moost go
To sinfonies, sonatas,
  Or an oratorio.
Vhen you dinks you knows 'pout musik,
  More ash any other man,
Be sure de soul of Deutschland
  Into your soul ish ran.

Will'st dou learn de Deutsche Sprache?
  Dou moost eat apout a peck
A week, of stinging sauerkraut,
  Und sefen pfoundts of speck.
Mit Gott knows vot in vinegar,
  Und deuce knows vot in rum:
Dis ish de only cerdain vay
  To make de accents coom.

Will'st dou learn de Deutsche Sprache?
  Brepare dein soul to shtand
Soosh sendences ash ne'er vas heardt
  In any oder land.
Till dou canst make parentheses
  Intwisted—ohne zahl—
Dann wirst du erst Deutschfertig seyn,*
  For a languashe ideál.

Will'st dou learn de Deutsche Sprache?
  Du must mitout an fear
Trink afery tay an gallon dry,
  Of foamin Sherman bier.
Und de more you trinks, pe certain,
  More Deutsch you 'll surely pe;
For Gambrinus ish de Emperor
  Of de whole of Germany.

* Then only you will be ready in German.

Will'st dou learn de Deutsche Sprache ?
  Be sholly, brav, und treu,
For dat veller ish kein Deutscher
  Who ish not a sholly poy.
Find out vot means Gemüthlichkeit,
  Und do it mitout fail,
In Sang und Klang dein Lebenlang,*
  A brick—ganz kreuzfidél.

Will'st dou learn de Deutsche Sprache ?
  If a shendleman dou art,
Denn shtrike right indo Deutschland,
  Und get a schveetes heart.
From Schwabenland or Sachsen
  Vhere now dis writer pees ;
Und de bretty girls all wachsen
  Shoost like aepples on de drees.

* In Music and Song all thy life long.

Boot if dou bee'st a laty
  Denn on de oder hand,
Take a blonde moustachioed lofer
  In de vine green Sherman land.
Und if you shoost kit married
  (Vood mit vood soon makes a vire),
O, denn you 'll find de Dutch vill come
  Ash fast ash you tesire.

LOVE SONG.

O, VERE mine lofe a sugar-powl,
De fery shmallest loomp
Vouldt shveet de seas, from pole to pole,
Und make de shildren shoomp.
Und if she vere a clofer-field,
I 'd bet my only pence,
It vould'nt pe no dime at all
Pefore I 'd shoomp de fence.

Her heafenly foice, it drill me so,
It oft-dimes seems to hoort,
She ish de holiest anamile
Dat roons oopon de dirt.
De renpow rises vhen she sings,
De sonnshine vhen she dalk ;
De angels crow und flop deir vings
Vhen she goes out to valk.

So livin white, so carnadine,
Mine lofe's gomblexion show ;
It 's shoost like Abendcarmosine,
Rich gleamin on de shnow.
Her soul makes plushes in her sheek
Ash sommer reds de wein,
Or sonnlight sends a fire life troo
An blank Karfunkelstein.

De überschwengliche idées
  Dis lofe poot in my mind,
Vouldt make a foost-rate philosoph
  Of any human kind.
'Tis schudderin schveet on eart to meet
  An himmlisch-hoellisch Qual;
Und treat mitwhiles to Kümmel Schnapps
  De Schœnheitsidéal.

GLOSSARY.

The reader would do well to consult the Glossaries of the three former collections.

Abendgold, (Ger.)—Evening gold.
Abendsonnenschein, (Ger.)—Evening sunshine.
Ach weh, (Ger.)—Oh, woe.
Allatag, (Ger. dial.)—Every day.
Allaweil, (Ger. dial.)—Always; also whilst.
Anamile, (Amer.)—Animal.
Antworded, (Ger.)—Answered.
Baender-box—Band-box.
Be-ghostet, (Ger. *Begeistert*)—Inspired.
Begreifen, (Ger.)—Understand.
Beheaded, *Behauptet*, (Ger.)—Asserted.
Bemoost, (Ger.)—Mossgrown, in student's language, *ein bemooste Haupt*, an old student.
Be-raised—Raised, with the augment, literal for Ger. *erhoben*.
Blitz, (Ger.)—Lightning.
Bole Jack road—Near Murfreesboro, Tennessee.
Bountiee (Amer.)—Bounty-money paid during the war as a premium to soldiers. To jump the bounty, was to secure the premium and then run away.

> "This is the song of Billy Jones,
> Who jumped the boun-ti-ee."
>
> —*American Ballad of* 1846.

Brav, (Ger.)—Good.
Brummed, (Ger. *Brummen*.)—To growl.
Bumming—From Bummer.
Bushwhackers—Guerillas.

Bust his shell—Broke his head.
Carmosine, (Ger.)—Crimson. French, *cramoisi*
Carnadine—Incarnadine.
Coster—The inventor of the art of printing, according to the Dutch.
Crislies—Grisly, (bear.)
Damit, (Ger.)—Therewith.
Deutschland—Germany.
Die wile es möhte leben—During all its life.

Daz wolde er immer dienen
Die wile es möhte leben.
Kutrun. XV. Aventiure, 756th verse.

Dooks—Ducks.
Druckerei—Printing-office.
Earnsthaft, ernsthaft—Serious.
Elders, (Ger. *Eltern*)—Parents.
Elfenbein, (Ger.)—Ivory.
Ergeben, (Ger.)—Resigned.
Error-dom, Irrthum—Error.
Euchred—From Euchre, a western game of cards.
Fass (Ger.)—Barrel.
Fore-by—Literal translation of the German *Vorbei.*
Fore-lying—Literal translation of *Vorliegend.*
Frau, (Ger.)—Woman.
Froze to de ready—Held fast to the money.
Fullenden —Vollenden.
Fuss, (Ger.)—Foot.
Fust—The partner of Gutemberg, the inventor of the art of printing.
Gast, (Ger.)—Guest.
Gauer—Vallies.
Gaul dern—A Yankee oath.
Gauner-sprache, (Ger.)—Thieves' language.
Geh hin mein Puch, (German of 16th century.)
Gekommen so, (Ger.)—Come thus.
Gemüthlichkeit, (Ger.)—Kindly disposition, good nature.
Gestohlen und bekannt, (Ger.)—Stolen, and known.
Glamour—Ocular deception by magic.
Goblum—For goblin.
Gotteshaus, (Ger.)—House of God.
Grillers—Guerillas.
Guve—Southern slang for give. *Guv*, for give, is also English slang as well as American.
Gutemberg—The inventor of the art of printing.
Heavy—Hood.
Heine, Heinrich—German poet.
Heini von Steier—Heinrich von Ofterdingen.

Hereauf, hierauf—Thereupon.
Her-re-liche, herrliche—Superb, grand, noble.
Herzlich, (Ger.)—Hearty.
Himmel, (Ger.)—Heaven.
Himmels-Potz-Pumpen-Herrgott—A mild sort of a German imprecation, untranslatable.
Himmlisch' hoellisch' qual, (Ger.)—Heavenly-hellish pain.
Hoof-irons; (*Huf-eisen* in Ger.)—Horse-shoe.
Hunk, (Amer.)—Stout, solid, profitable. "To be all hunk" means to come out of a speculation with advantage. To be well off.
I Gili romaneskro—This song is written in the German gipsy dialect. *Eh!* in third line of second verse, is the German word *ehe*, "ere," or before. *Kuribente* ("in war,") is in the Slavonic and gipsy *local* case, or as Pott calls it (*Die Zigeuner in Europa und Asien*) the Second Dative.
In Sang und Klang dein Leben lang, (Ger.)—In music and song all thy life long.
Jeff—A game played by throwing up types, generally for "refreshments."
Kalt, (Ger.)—Cold.
Karfunkelstein, (Ger.)—Carbuncle.
Kauder-Waelsch, (Ger.)—Gibberish.
Kitin, a kitin—Flying or running rapidly.
Kanaster, (Ger.)—Canaster tobacco.
Kümmel, (Ger.)—Cumin brandy.
Lavergne—A place between Nashville and Murfreesboro', in the state of Tennessee.
Lieder, Lieds, (Ger.)—Songs.
Like spiders down their webs—Breitmann's soldiers are supposed to have been expert turners or gymnasts.
Loafer, (Amer.)—A term which, considered as the German pronunciation of *lover*, is a close translation of *rom*, since this latter means both a gipsy and a husband.
Loudet, (*Lauten* in Ger.)—To make sound.
Lumpenglocke—An abusive term applied to bells, especially to those which are rung to give notice that the beer-houses must close.
Mit hoontin knife, &c. :—

"With her white hands so lovely,
She dug the Count his grave.
From her dark eyes sad weeping,
The holy water she gave."

Old German Ballad.

Mohr, ein schwarzer, (Ger.)—A blackamoor.
Morgan—John Morgan, a notorious Confederate guerilla during the late war in America.

Moskopolite, (Amer.)—Cosmopolite. Mossyhead is the German student phrase for an old student.
Mutter, (Ger.)—Mother.
Noth, (Ger.)—Need, dire extremity. Das war des Breitmann's Noth. That was Breitmann's sore trial. Imitated from the last line of *The Nibelungen Lied.*
Nun endlich, (Ger.)—Now at last.
O'Brady—An Irish giant commemorated in an old popular song.
Odenwald—A thickly-wooded district in South Germany.
On-belongs—Literal translation of *Zugehört.*
Oop-sproong—For *aufsprung.*
Orgel-ton, (Ger.)—Organ sound.
Out-sprach—Outspoke.
Peeps—People. "Hard on the American peeps"—a phrase for anything exacting or severely pressing.
Pestain—Stain, with the augment.
Pfaelzer—A man from the Rhenish Palatinate.
Pie the forms—Break and scatter the forms of types—the greatest disaster conceivable to a true typo.
Pig-sticker—Bowie-knife.
Pile out, (Amer.)—Hurry out.
Plug-muss—Fight for a fire-plug. American fireman's language.
Poonkin—Pumpkin.
Red cock—Or make de red cock crow. Einem den rothen Hahn auf's Dach setzen. A German proverb signifying to set fire to a house.
Rede, (Ger.)—Speech.
Red-Waelsch, Roth-Waelsch, (Ger.)—Thieves' language.
Reiter, (Ger.)—Rider.
Ridersmann, (*Reitersmann* in Ger.)—Rider.
Ritter, (Ger.)—Knight.
Sachsen—Saxonia, Saxony.
Sacrin—Consecrating.
Sauerkraut, (Ger.)—Pickled cabbage.
Scatterin, Scotterin—Scattering.
Schauer, (Ger.)—Awe.
Schenk aus, (Ger.)—Pour out.
Schimmel, (Ger.)—Grey horse.
Schloss, (Ger.)—Castle.
Schönheitsidéal, (Ger.)—The ideal of beauty.
Schopenhauer—A celebrated German "philosophical physiologist.
Schwaben—Suabia.
Schwan, (Ger.)—Swan.
Scrouged, (Amer.)—Pressed, jammed.
Seelen—Ideal. Soul's ideal.
Shapel—Chapel is an old word for a printing-office.
Shipsy—Gipsy.
Shlide—Slide. "Let it slide," vulgar for "let it go."

Shooting-stick—A shooting-stick is used for closing up the form of types.
Sonntag, (Ger.)—Sunday.
Speck, (Ger.)—Bacon.
Spiel, (Ger.)—Play.
Sporn, (Ger.)—Spur.
Stim, (Ger. *Stimme*)—Voice.
Sturm und Drang, (Ger.)—Literally Storm and violence. *Sturm und Drangperiode*, signifying a particular period of German literature.
Sweynheim and Pannartz—The first printers at Rome.
Takes—Allotments of copy to each printer.
Thrip, (Southern Amer.)—Threepence.
Todt, (Ger.)—Dead.
Treppe—Stairs.
Treu, (Ger.)—Faithful, true.
Ueberschwengliche, (Ger.)—Transcendental, elevated.
Verdammt, (Ger.)—D—d.
Wachsen, (Ger.)—To grow.

> " Komm' ich in's galante Sachsen
> Wo die schöne Maedchen wachsen."
> —*Old German Song*.

Wald, (Ger.)—Wood.
We'uns, you'ns—We and 'you. A common vulgarism through the Southern States.

> " 'Tis sad that we'uns from you'ns parts
> When you'ns hev stolen we'uns' hearts."

Wild und Weh, (Ger.)—Wild and woebegone.
Wo bist du? (Ger.)—Where art?
Woe-moaedy, (Ger. *Wehmüthig*)—Moanful, doleful.
Wohlauf, (Ger.)—Well, come on, cheer up.
Wurst—A German student word for indifference.
Yarttausend, Jahrtausend—A thousand years.
Yellow pine—Mulatto.

> " I lost a maiden in that hour."—*Byron*.

Yungling, Jüngling, (Ger.)—Youth.

PRINTED BY BALLANTYNE AND COMPANY
EDINBURGH AND LONDON

Price 1s.

SECOND SERIES.

HANS BREITMANN'S CHRISTMAS

With other Ballads.

1. Hans Breitmann's Christmas.
2. Der Freischütz.
3. Breitmann about Town.
4. Weingeist.
5. Schnitzerl's Philosopede. Part 1.
6. Schnitzerl's Philosopede. Part 2.

www.ingramcontent.com/pod-product-compliance
Lightning Source LLC
Chambersburg PA
CBHW020334090426
42735CB00009B/1540
9783741181627